# 1

## The Portrait of Christ: human yet triumphant

'The central figure of Christ dominates the painting, not only because of his imposing size but also because of the light which emanates from his body,' notes Fr van Asseldonk. This light shines over all the attendant figures. The red and black colours of the actual cross accentuate his luminous body.

According to some commentators, the black behind his extended arms represents the empty tomb. The figures gazing into the tomb, at either end of Jesus' outstretched arms, may be angels or perhaps two of the women who came to the tomb early in the morning to anoint the body of Jesus (*Mark* 16:1). Some suggest they are Peter and the Beloved Disciple surrounding the face of Jesus, the angels and the long, almost staff-like cross that the victorious Jesus holds.

The cross of San Damiano, painted on linen glued to a cross made of walnut, is a fine example of an Italian painted cross. Just as it spoke to Francis, this cross has something to tell us in the great detail of its ornamentation and design.

their foundation. When they left San Damiano in 1257, they took the crucifix with them and have preserved it carefully ever since. It is venerated by thousands of visitors to Assisi every year. It is currently housed in the Church of Santa Chiara (St Clare). Since 1958 it has been hung in a place accessible to pilgrims.

Replicas of the crucifix are present in many Franciscan houses, in churches and in private homes throughout the world.

This crucifix stands 2.1 metres high (6 feet 10 inches) and 1.3 metres wide (4 feet 3 inches). It was painted in the twelfth century by an unknown Umbrian artist. By the first half of that century, Italian artists were painting crosses on wooden panels which were broadened in certain places (for example, under the arms of Christ) to provide a larger surface on which to paint various figures and small subsidiary scenes from the life of Christ.

The style of these painted crosses is Romanesque, but they also reveal a strong Byzantine influence, perhaps influenced by the Syriac rite monks who lived for centuries around Spoleto, Italy. Some Byzantine characteristics are the hair completely

# Introduction

The San Damiano crucifix is possibly the best known and venerated crucifix in the world. In 1206 it was probably hanging above the altar in the apse of the abandoned Chapel of San Damiano, just outside Assisi, in the Umbrian region of Italy. It would have been the central feature in the small, neglected chapel in which the Blessed Sacrament would not have been reserved.

A young man, Francis Bernadone, entered the chapel. Kneeling to pray, he heard a voice coming from the crucifix say three times, 'Francis, go and repair my house which, as you see, is falling completely into ruin.' It was a moment of ecstasy and great consolation for Francis. He had received from God a mission, a vocation. He left the San Damiano Chapel irrevocably transformed.

This icon cross which spoke to Francis has been in the care of the Poor Clare Sisters since the time Francis took them to San Damiano shortly after

# Contents

THE CRUCIFIX THAT SPOKE TO ST FRANCIS
Text © Michael Goonan 2000

First published 2000
Second edition (hardcover) published 2007

National Library of Australia
Cataloguing-in-Publication Data:
    Goonan, Michael G. (Michael Gerard)
    The crucifix that spoke to St Francis.
    2nd ed.

    ISBN 978 1 921032 23 3

    1. Francis, of Assisi, Saint, 1182-1226.  2. Chapel of San
    Damiano (Assisi, Italy).  3. Crosses - Italy - Assisi.  I. Title.
    246.558094565

AUSTRALIAN edition published by
St Pauls Publications
PO Box 906, Strathfield NSW 2135, Australia
ISBN 978 1 921032 23 3

NORTH AMERICAN edition published by
ST PAULS, Alba House
2187 Victory Blvd, Staten Island NY 10314, USA
ISBN 978-0-8189-1242-9

Illustration of San Damaino crucifix © Photo Scala, Florence. Reproduced with permission. Illustration of St Francis on page 27: detail from a fresco in San Damiano Monastery – photo by De Canale © Periodici San Paolo, Italy. Reproduced with permission.

Design and layout by Kylie Prats and Geraldine Lian

Printed by Everbest Printing Co Ltd, China

ST PAULS is an activity of the priests and brothers of the Society of St Paul who place at the centre of their lives the mission of evangelisation through the means of social communication.

# The Crucifix
# that Spoke to St Francis

Michael Goonan, SSP

ST PAULS

# The Crucifix
# that Spoke to St Francis

(*John* 20:3-9). However this is unlikely as Peter is traditionally portrayed with a short beard.

Clearly the painter is not representing the very moment of the death of Jesus. The body depicted is not a bloody corpse hanging on a gibbet. It is a living body, indeed a body that radiates the fullness of God. What we see is the majestic Son of God, who has triumphed over suffering and death. Instead of a crown of thorns, he wears a halo of glory with a triumphal cross. With arms outstretched he is in the act of ascending into heaven.

This is further emphasised by the Christ-in-Ascension scene depicted at the top of the cross. In this scene the triumphant Christ is being welcomed into heaven by the angels. He has the trophy of the glorious cross in his left hand (the cross seems so slight compared with the glory of his victory).

His right hand is raised towards the hand of his heavenly Father. Michael Scanlon, TOR, author of *The San Damiano Cross: An explanation*, says that the Father's hand is offering 'the blessing of God the Father on all that Jesus has done.' The raised index finger on the Father's hand speaks to us of the Holy Spirit–'finger of God's right hand', as we sing in the *Veni Creator Spiritus.*

While depicting a triumphant Christ, the artist certainly acknowledges the passion of Christ. The marks of crucifixion are clearly seen in his bleeding wounds. But this Christ is not hanging on the cross as a man of sorrows. He is portrayed without pain. The Christ depicted here has already overcome suffering and death.

Thus, while the passion is acknowledged, what is portrayed on this crucifix is the triumphant redeemer whose divinity is clearly emphasised. But the humanity of Christ also emerges in this painting. For instance, the head of Christ, emphasised by the raised halo, radiates much tenderness in the almond-shaped eyes and the half smile. Also, Christ's head is slightly tilted, a very human gesture.

Again, though presented as a triumphant Christ, he is clearly not portrayed as a king. Rather he wears the loincloth of a poor man. His arms are not rigid, but bent in a prayerful, supplicatory posture.

The deep affection many Franciscans and others continue to have for this crucifix is further testimony to the humanity of Christ that emerges in this painting. Sister Mary Seraphim, a Poor Clare writing in 1980, looked at it and sensed an almost infinite sadness in the eyes of Christ: 'These eyes compel us. We are bidden to look at the vast sweep of salvation, but also to experience the sad yearnings of a saviour over a world that rejected his love.' Her observations on what she called 'The Miraculous Crucifix of San Damiano' show how the human dimension of Christ is realised in this depiction and is at the heart of its continuing appeal.

The San Damiano crucifix was, in fact, painted at a time when a significant transformation was taking place in the presentation of Christ in spirituality and art. In the preceding centuries great emphasis had been placed on the divinity of Christ. In the period into which Francis was born a much greater appreciation of the humanity of Christ was emerging. Francis, who deeply loved the poor man from Nazareth, was to play a major role in this movement. Through the creation of the nativity scene he highlighted the humble birth of Jesus in a stable in Bethlehem. He also drew attention to the suffering that Jesus endured on the cross for love of us. The crucifixes that were painted in Franciscan churches in the thirteenth century no longer portrayed a triumphant Christ but Christ crucified, head bowed in death and swaying from the cross.

Painted during this time of transition, the San Damiano crucifix portrays a living triumphant Christ but, as we have noted, the humanising elements characteristic of the age are also present. While the humanity and the divinity of Christ are expressed in this crucifix we must, of course, note with Fr van Asseldonk that Christ 'is contemplated in the unity of his person, instead of in the diversity of his two natures.' It is the one Christ, human and divine, whom we meet through this icon.

This crucifix is unique in that it reveals the whole paschal mystery of Christ—suffering, death, resurrection and glorious ascension. It is no wonder that Francis was attracted to the Christ of the San Damiano crucifix.

# 2

# The Attendant Figures: Christ's companions in life and art

It is the Christ of the Gospel of John who is portrayed in this crucifix. This Christ is the light of the world and is in control throughout his passion. He announces from the cross the salvation of the world with the words, 'It is finished' (*John* 19:30). In the painting we find the words 'Jesus of Nazareth, the king of the Jews' inscribed in Latin above the head of Christ. Only in John's Gospel is the word 'Nazareth' included in the inscription on the cross (19:19).

The Christ in John's Gospel does not die alone, abandoned by all. Rather, he dies in communion with God, and with dear companions nearby. In the cross of San Damiano these companions are painted in the panels under Christ's outstretched arms.

At the right side of Jesus are Mary, his mother, and the Beloved Disciple. This could be the moment when Jesus says, 'Woman, behold your son' (*John* 19:26).

Blood flows over the Beloved Disciple from the wound in Christ's side. He is a symbol of the Church redeemed by the blood of Christ. Following a Syrian tradition that dates from the sixth century, the blood is flowing from the *right* side of Christ.

Occupying a special place on the left side of Jesus is Mary of Magdala and beside her is Mary, the wife of Clopas (*John* 19:25). Like Mary, the mother of Jesus,

Mary of Magdala has her left hand raised to her chin. This is a classic Byzantine artistic formula expressing confusion and the struggle of human reason before the mystery of faith. Through this gesture the artist is alluding to the grief and turmoil these women must have felt as they witnessed the death of Jesus.

The attendant figures in this painting have, however, also witnessed the resurrection of Jesus. While the raised hands of Mary, the mother of Jesus, and Mary of Magdala speak of distress at Jesus' death, their faces reflect joy and lively faith in Christ. Indeed, gestures of joy far outweigh expressions of grief in this painting. Mary's gaze is not on the body of Jesus but on the Beloved Disciple. She is fulfilling her role as mother of the Church. Together with the Beloved Disciple and the women, Mary stands as a witness to the resurrection.

Next to the two women on Jesus left is a very interesting character, a centurion wearing a knee-length Roman tunic. Maintaining a Johannine theme some commentators see him as the centurion who begged Jesus to heal his son (see *John* 4:46-54). The head just visible behind the centurion is said to be that of the healed son.

That may be the case, but I prefer the suggestion that the centurion is the one mentioned in Mark's Gospel who, having witnessed Jesus' death, declares 'Truly this man was the Son of God' (*Mark* 15:19). In this latter interpretation, the small head behind the centurion is probably the face of the artist. This was a commonly accepted way for artists to autograph their work and, in this case, to be immortalised as a witness to Christ. Lines above the artist's head suggest a crowd of people, also witnesses to the wondrous events of Christ's passion, death and resurrection.

Significantly, three fingers of the centurion's hand are in the traditional iconographic sign for 'I am speaking'. In a Christian context this means, 'I am testifying that Jesus is Lord.' Like the Beloved Disciple and the three women he too is a witness to the resurrection of Christ. His insertion is surprising if the painter is indeed working from John's Gospel and, therefore, reflects the painter's appreciation of the universal character of Christ's saving activity. Christ is the saviour of all people.

Continuing the theme of universalism, two small figures are depicted below the major scenes. Beneath Mary and the Beloved Disciple is the Roman soldier who pierced Jesus' side with a lance (*John* 19:35). This soldier, who in Christian tradition has been given the name Longinus, is depicted holding the lance.

At the foot of the centurion on Jesus' left is the soldier who offered Jesus the sponge soaked in wine (*John* 19:29). Christian tradition calls him Stephaton (faulty derivation of the Greek for sponge). He certainly would have been painted holding a staff and sponge to balance the spear of Longinus. They are no longer visible.

Interestingly, the blood flowing down Christ's arms and dripping at the elbows will fall on these two men who played a role in Jesus' death. Christ's redeeming love flows even on those who 'look upon him whom they have pierced' (*John* 19:37).

Beside the left calf of Jesus is a small rooster, a reminder of the betrayal of Jesus by Peter. I find significant the fact that the rooster is so small. Sin is a reality of which we need to be wary, but the salvation of Christ is so much greater than the power of human sin.

The figures at the bottom of the cross are no longer clearly discernible. I personally like the suggestion that these figures represent the patriarchs and the holy people of the Old Testament who had to wait in the nether world for the coming of the Saviour. Saving blood from the wounds in Christ's feet flows over these people who preceeded Jesus in time.

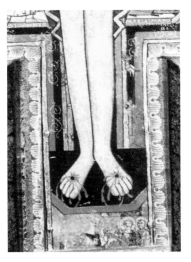

In this reading of the scene the black space surrounding Jesus' feet symbolises the hell into which Jesus descended, according to the Apostles' Creed, before rising and ascending into heaven, taking the just with him.

Though this interpretation of the scene at the foot of the cross is appealing, some commentators consider it to be highly unlikely. They suggest that the figures are most likely the principal saints of the Umbrian region: St Damian, St Rufinus, St Michael, St John the Baptist, St Peter and St Paul.

Finally, two angels are painted under each of the outstretched arms of Christ. They are in animated conversation, perhaps marvelling at the wonderful events depicted in the painting. Saving blood from the wounds of Christ's hands flow over them also. By his paschal mystery Christ is the saviour of all creation. Ten more angels crowd around the ascended Christ at the top of the crucifix. His right hand is raised in greeting, and five of the angels have their own hands extended in a gesture of welcome.

Truly, this crucifix expresses not only the total and universal paschal mystery of Christ, but invites everyone to participate in it in lively faith. Gazing upon it we, like Francis, are drawn into the community of witnesses to this great event.

# 3

## The Crucifix Speaks
## of Joy and Community in Christ

The San Damiano crucifix may well have influenced the spiritual development of Francis in at least two ways.

*First*, as already noted, this crucifix expresses little grief or pain in its depiction of the paschal mystery of Christ. The joy evoked by Christ's resurrection and ascension far outweighs the grief caused by his death. This is also reflected in Francis' personal experience of the paschal mystery. For Francis, the cross in any form is a source of great pain, but also a source of joy because of the salvation that flows from it. Shortly before his death, Francis urged his followers to pray: 'We adore you, Lord Jesus Christ, in all your churches throughout the world, and we bless you, for through your holy cross you have redeemed the world.'

Francis truly experienced joy in his encounter with the passion of Christ. He left his encounter with the cross of San Damiano 'totally filled with divine consolation,' writes St Clare in her *Testament*. Thomas of Celano makes a similar point in his *Second Life* of Francis. His encounter with the crucified at San Damiano was an experience of divine love that made him want to cry and sing at the same time.

The same experience of intense suffering and great joy happened when Francis received the stigmata, the wounds of Jesus, in his own hands, feet and side. Thus, the joyful aspect of the paschal mystery—an encounter with overwhelming saving love—expressed in the cross of San Damiano also characterised Francis' experience of the passion of Christ.

*Second*, the communal dimension apparent in the cross of San Damiano is also noticeable in the spirituality of Francis. What is highlighted in this crucifix is the communion of the crucified and risen Lord with his whole Church, with the angels and the saints. Many who have prayed before this crucifix have felt themselves sharers in this communion.

The Christ on this crucifix is not abandoned. Paradoxically, in 1206, the crucifix rested in the abandoned church of San Damiano, and Francis, who was also abandoned, visited it. He had not found a calling and was in some ways alone in his quest. Difficulties, especially with his father, were already present. In his encounter with the Christ of San Damiano he experienced a call, a mission, a vocation. He was no longer abandoned. Integral to his call was a sense of community and communion in Christ and in Christ's passion. This sense of communion extended not only to all human beings, but also to the birds of the air, the sun, the moon, indeed, all of creation.

The cross of San Damiano still connects people to community. In many places throughout the world people of all ages gather regularly around a replica of the cross of San Damiano for a time of prayer, following the practice of the Taize community in France. Community is expressed in worship and praise of the Christ of the cross of San Damiano.

In the joyful aspect the paschal mystery and in the feelings of community evoked by the crucifix, we find realities that were also visible in the life of St Francis. The San Damiano crucifix is very appropriately situated within the Franciscan spiritual tradition and, indeed, within the great tradition of Christian spirituality. The crucifix that spoke to St Francis in 1206 continues to speak to us today.

# References

In preparing the text of this booklet, the author was helped by Fr Michael Guinan OFM, of the Franciscan School of Theology, Berkeley, California, and by the following works which are not easily accessible:

Gagnon, Dominique, 'The Christ of San Damiano: Its spiritual meaning' *FIA Contact* 3/3 (1982) pp. 2-11.

Scanlon, Michael TOR, *The San Damiano Cross: An explanation*, Stubenville, OH: Franciscan University Press, 1983.

Schmidt, T. Anne, SFCC, SFO, 'The Cross of San Damiano Still Speaks' *The Cord* (1988) pp. 69-77.

Serpahim, Sister Mary, PCPA 'The Miraculous Crucifix of San Damiano' *The Cord* (1980) pp. 215-218.

van Asseldonk, Optatus OFM Cap, 'The San Damiano Crucifix' *Stigmata News* Vol 1 No 10 (October, 1982). This is an abbreviated translation of 'Il Crocifisso Di San Damiano: Visto e Vissuto da S. Francesco' *Laurentianum* 22 (1981) pp. 453-476.

Further information on the San Damiano crucifix, prepared by Brother Jim Cronley OFMCap, can be found at this website:

http://www.capuchinfriars.org.au/sandam.html

Prayers of St Francis

# Before the San Damiano Crucifix

Most High,

glorious God,

enlighten the darkness of my heart.

Give me, Lord,

a correct faith,

a certain hope,

a perfect charity,

sense and knowledge,

that I may carry out

your holy and true decree.

# For Holy Thursday

We adore, you, Lord Jesus Christ

in all your churches throughout the world,

and we bless you,

because by your holy cross

you have redeemed the world.

# Canticle of the Creatures

Most high, omnipotent, good Lord,
to you alone belong praise and glory,
all honour and blessing,
and no one is worthy to speak your name.

Be you praised, my Lord,
in all your creatures,
and especially in Brother Sun,
who lightens up the day for us,
who is fine and radiant with great splendour.
He is an image of you, Most High.

Be you praised, my Lord,
through our Sister Moon and the stars
whom you have made clear-shining
and precious and beautiful.

Be you praised, my Lord,
through Brother Wind
and through the air and clouds
and fine days and all weathers,
through whom you give food
to all your creatures.

Be you praised, my Lord,
through Sister Water
for she is very useful and humble,
precious and pure.

Be you praised, my Lord,
through Brother Fire
through whom you light up the night,
who is beautiful and joyous,
powerful and strong.

Be you praised, my Lord,
through our sister, Mother Earth,
who sustains us and governs us,
and who brings forth
different fruits and flowers
and useful plants.

Be you praised, my Lord,
through those who grant pardon
for love of you,
through those who are patient in sickness and trial.
Blessed are they who endure in peace;
by you, most high, they shall be crowned.

Be you praised, my Lord,
through our Sister, Bodily Death,
whom no one living can escape.
Alas for those who die in mortal sin;
blessed are those
who do your most holy will,
for the second death shall not harm them.

Praise and bless God and give God thanks;
and serve God with great humility.

# Instrument of God's peace

Lord, make me an instrument of your peace:
where there is hatred, let me sow love;
where there is injury, pardon;
where there is doubt, faith;
where there is despair, hope;
where there is darkness, light;
where there is sadness, joy.

Divine Master,
grant that I may not so much seek
to be consoled, as to console;
to be understood, as to understand;
to be loved as to love.
for it is in giving that we receive,
it is in pardoning that we are pardoned,
and in dying that we are brought to
        eternal life.